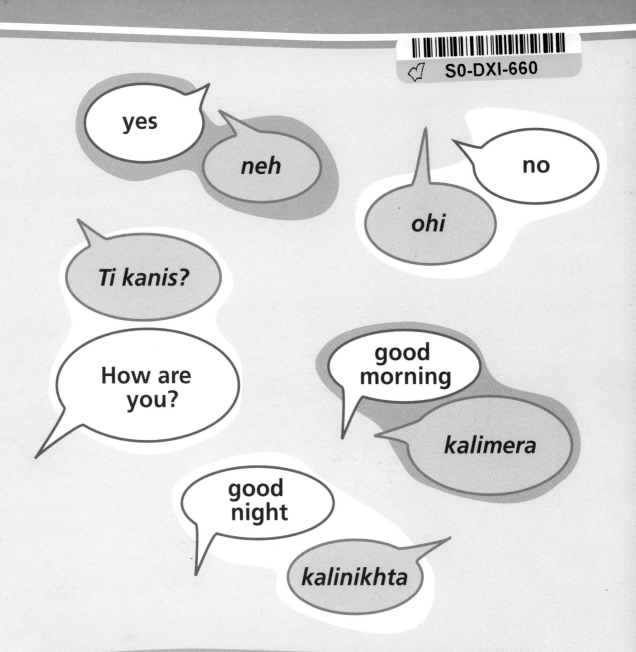

Welcome to
Greece

Meredith Costain   Paul Collins

This edition first published in 2002 in the United States of America by Chelsea House Publishers,
a subsidiary of Haights Cross Communications

Chelsea House Publishers
1974 Sproul Road, Suite 400
Broomall, PA 19008–0914

The Chelsea House world wide web address is www.chelseahouse.com

Library of Congress Cataloging-in-Publication Data Applied for.
ISBN 0-7910-6545-6

First published in 2000 by
Macmillan Education Australia Pty Ltd
627 Chapel Street, South Yarra, Australia, 3141

Copyright © Meredith Costain and Paul Collins 2000

Edited by Miriana Dasovic
Text design and page layout by Goanna Graphics (Vic) Pty Ltd
Cover design by Goanna Graphics (Vic) Pty Ltd
Maps by Stephen Pascoe
Illustrations by Vaughan Duck
Printed in Hong Kong

Acknowledgements
The author and the publisher are grateful to the following for permission to reproduce
copyright material:

Cover photograph: Farmer and donkey, © Blaine Harrington.

Blaine Harrington pp. 5–15, 18, 19, 22, 23, 25–8; Lonely Planet Images, p. 24 © Leanne Logan,
pp. 21, 29 © Neil Setchfield, p. 20 © David Tipling; PhotoDisc p. 30.

While every care has been taken to trace and acknowledge copyright the publishers tender their
apologies for any accidental infringement where copyright has proved untraceable.

Contents

Welcome to Greece!

Yiassou! My name is Alexander. I live on Mykonos, an island in the Aegean Sea.

Greece is in southern Europe. We have borders to the north and east with Albania, Bulgaria, Turkey and the former Yugoslav Republic of Macedonia. Our shores are washed by four different stretches of water: the Sea of Crete, the Mediterranean Sea, the Aegean Sea and the Ionian Sea.

Greece is made up of many islands. No part of Greece is more than about 100 kilometers (62 miles) from the sea, even on the mainland. Our coastline is the longest in Europe. People come from all over the world to visit our beautiful beaches and to enjoy our sunny weather.

Our flag has four white and five blue stripes, with a white cross in the top left-hand corner. Blue and white are Greece's national colors. White stands for the purity of the struggle for Greek independence in 1821, and blue is for the sea and sky. The cross represents the Greek Orthodox Church.

That's me, with my younger brother and sister.

Family life

My island, Mykonos, is one of the most beautiful places in the world. It has dazzling white houses, a sparkling blue sea, and a cloudless blue sky. People call it the 'jewelry box'.

My family lives in the port area, called Hora. Our little house is white, like all the other buildings here. Long ago, a king ordered all the people to paint their houses white. Now it has become a custom to whitewash our house with **lime** every summer. We paint the doors and window frames blue.

The port of Mykonos, my home town.

I have a younger brother called Con, and two younger sisters, Voula and baby Despina. Both my parents work in the tourist industry. My father, Tassos, works as a tourist guide. My mother, Efi, sells postcards and souvenirs in a gift shop.

After school, Con and I often talk to the fishermen in the port. One day, I hope to have my own boat!

*My grandmother, **Yaya**, with my baby sister, Despina. Yaya lives with us. She looks after Voula and Despina while my mother is at work. Yaya wears only black clothes. It is a sign of respect for my grandfather, who died last year.*

My father guides visitors through the narrow streets of our village, and takes them to see our famous windmills.

School

Most Greek children go to kindergarten when they are three-and-a-half. Two years later they start primary school, which they attend for six years. After grade 6, they study for three years at a school called a *gymnasium*. Students can then choose to go to a *lyceum* for three years, to prepare for college or university, or to go to a technical school. Exams are held at the end of grades 11 and 12.

My school day starts at 8:30 a.m. and finishes at 2:30 p.m. Our teacher is very strict and always makes us work hard. He gives us lots of homework, too. My subjects include modern Greek, maths, geography, history, art, music and religion. Every student in Greece learns religion at school. I love learning about all our **myths** and legends. My favorite legend is about Jason and the Golden Fleece.

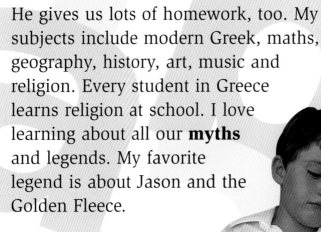

The grandmothers in our village sometimes come to our school and help us with our reading.

Sports and leisure

Our love of sport goes back to ancient times. The first recorded Olympic Games were held in 776 BC, but athletic games had been held at Olympia as early as 1370 BC. These games were religious ceremonies in honor of the god Zeus. Young men raced a distance of about 185 meters (607 feet), which is the length of a stadium.

Today, soccer is our most popular sport. We call it *podosphéro*. There are large stadiums in Athens and other major cities. Many people say the only time our streets are empty is when the national soccer team's match is being shown on TV!

Basketball and volleyball are also popular sports. Because Greek people live so close to the sea, many of us enjoy water sports. Children learn to swim when they are very young. Adults enjoy sailing, diving, rowing and yacht racing.

Thousands of people gather every year to watch our famous car race, the Acropolis Rally.

In the evenings, many people like to sit outside in street cafés and listen to music played on the *bouzouki*. This is a stringed instrument shaped like a small guitar.

Pavement cafés are a popular place to spend leisure time. This one is in Iraklion, on Crete. Thousands of years ago, young people came to Crete from many different countries to perform in bull-dances.

Greek culture

We are very proud of our culture, which is thousands of years old. The period from 461–431 BC is known as the 'Golden Age'. During this time, **playwrights** such as Aeschylus, Euripides and Aristophanes produced plays that made people think about their lives. Their plays are still performed and studied around the world. Philosophy, which is the study of ideas and knowledge, was also developed at this time. Our famous philosophers include Socrates, Plato and Aristotle.

Our language is the oldest in Europe. Many Greek words have become part of other languages. Homer is our greatest poet. He wrote the *Iliad* and the *Odyssey* around 700 BC. These are long poems that tell of the heroic deeds of gods and men. Modern Greek writers include the poet George Seferis, who won the Nobel Prize for Literature, and Nikos Kazantzakis, who wrote the book *Zorba the Greek*. It has been turned into a famous movie.

The open-air theater at Epidaurus, in the northeast Peloponnese, was built over 2,000 years ago. A drama festival is held here every year.

The ancient Greeks were also fine artists. Much of their work was painted on pottery or on the walls of buildings. During the **Classical Period**, they built many beautiful temples for the gods. These include the Temple of Nike, and the Temple of Zeus in Olympia. Today, our craftwork is among the finest in the world, especially our hand-painted pottery and jewelry.

Music has always been an important part of our culture. The English word 'music' comes from the Greek word *mousike*. In many villages, folk music is played on hand-made instruments, such as the bouzouki. *Rembetika*, a type of traditional singing, is very popular. We have hundreds of different dances. Most of them are performed by a group of people who dance arm-in-arm in a line or open circle. People dance at weddings, festivals, or just for the fun of it!

An ancient painting found at Knossos, Crete.

Bouzouki players in Kritsa, Crete.

Festivals and religion

Nearly all Greeks are Greek Orthodox, which is a form of Christianity. The word Orthodox means 'right-believing'. My family goes to church every Sunday. Sometimes the service lasts three hours! The church in our village is very traditional. The men stand on one side, and the women on the other. During the service, *Yaya* walks around the church, kissing the **icons** on the walls. Icons are paintings of holy people such as Jesus, Mary and the saints. We also have icons in our house.

We have many religious feast days. Greek Christian names usually come from the names of saints. We celebrate our Saint's Day rather than our birthday. Villages also have their own festival, called *panayiri*, in memory of their patron saint.

Our most important religious days are Christmas and Easter. On Christmas Eve, my mother bakes sweet loaves called *christopsomo*. They are known as 'Christ bread'. We do not give presents at Christmas. Instead we wait until the feast of Saint Basil on New Year's Day.

A religious procession on the island of Santorini.

The celebration of Easter in spring lasts up to 10 weeks. It begins with Carnival, about three weeks before **Lent**. We parade donkeys through the streets, bang drums and collect money. People disguise themselves in masks and costumes, and dance in the streets.

The 15th of August is an important holiday throughout Greece. Thousands of pilgrims go to the Panaghia Evangelistria church on the island of Tinos. There they celebrate the day of the Virgin Mary, known as Assumption Day. We celebrate our independence from Turkey on the 25th of March, and *Ohi* Day on the 28th of October. *Ohi* means 'No' in Greek. This festival marks the day in 1940 when our prime minister told Italy's prime minister, Benito Mussolini, that his troops could not enter our country.

Greek festivals and holidays

Feast of Saint Basil	January 1
Epiphany	January 6
Independence Day	March 25
Easter	March/April
May Day	May 1
Assumption Day	August 15
Ohi Day ('No' Day)	October 28
Christmas Day	December 25

Greek Orthodox monks at Mt Athos.

Food and shopping

Greek food is known all over the world. We use fresh ingredients, spices and herbs. Olive oil is used in most of our dishes. Our climate is mild, so we can grow our vegetables naturally, without using chemicals. This means they always taste wonderful! Traditional Greek cooking uses herbs such as oregano, thyme, rosemary and spearmint.

Breakfast is usually only a light meal. We have bread and jam, and sheep's milk yogurt with honey. My father has only a cup of strong coffee before he leaves for work! Lunch is our main meal. We usually have grilled lamb or fish, served with a traditional salad. It is made from lettuce, tomatoes, olives and goat's cheese. We also have fresh fruit. For supper we will have something light, perhaps a salad, and dips served with pita bread. My favorite food is baklava, a sweet cake made from nuts and honey.

A family gathers for an outdoor meal.

Eating with friends is always fun. Greek cooks can spend days preparing a meal for a family or social gathering. Our parents love to have a Greek liqueur called ouzo, or a local wine with their meal. Sometimes we go out to a *taverna* to eat. We go into the kitchen, look at what is cooking, and make our choice.

We might choose moussaka, made with eggplant and minced meat, or fried squid. Sometimes we have *souvlakia*, which is marinated meat cooked on a skewer.

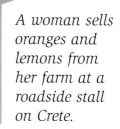

A woman sells oranges and lemons from her farm at a roadside stall on Crete.

Fish is a large part of our diet because we live so close to the sea. People buy fish from the markets or straight from the boats at the jetty.

Make souvlakia

Sizzling lamb kebabs taste delicious when cooked on a barbecue.

Ask an adult to help you prepare this dish.

You will need:

- 4 tablespoons olive oil
- juice of 1 lemon
- 1 teaspoon dried oregano
- salt and pepper
- 750 grams (1 1/2 lbs) lean lamb
- 1 onion, peeled
- 1 red pepper, 1 green pepper
- pita bread
- shredded lettuce
- diced tomato
- plain yogurt

What to do:

1 Mix the olive oil, lemon juice, salt, pepper and oregano to make a marinade for the lamb.

2 Cut the lamb into small cubes. Put the cubes in a bowl. Pour the marinade over them.

3 Leave the lamb in the fridge for at least four hours.

4 Chop the onion and peppers into chunks.

5 Thread the lamb, onion and peppers onto skewers.

6 Grill or barbecue the kebabs for 15 minutes.

7 Take the kebabs off the skewers. Place each kebab in the center of a piece of pita bread. Add some lettuce, tomato and yogurt.

8 Roll up the pita bread, and eat!

Make a calendar for Lent

For many years, people used to make their own calendars to help them keep track of the seven weeks leading to Easter. They cut out the shape of a nun with folded arms and seven feet. The nun had no mouth. This helped to remind people they were supposed to fast during Lent. Every Saturday, one of the nun's feet was torn off to show that a week had passed.

fold in

fold in

You will need:

- colored card
- a pencil
- scissors
- scraps of wool
- glue
- colored pencils or felt pens

What to do:

1 Draw a shape on the colored card like the one shown. Cut it out.

2 Draw a face on your nun. Remember not to give her a mouth!

3 Glue some scraps of wool to your nun's head. This will be her hair.

4 Draw flowers or some other design on your nun's skirt.

5 Fold your nun's arms inward so that her hands overlap.

6 On the Saturday of the first week of Lent, tear off the nun's first foot. Keep tearing off one foot each week until there are none left. Happy Easter!

Landscape and climate

Greece is divided into nine geographic regions. In the north are Thrace, Macedonia and Epirus. Thessaly, Central Greece and the Peloponnese are in the south. There are also three island regions. These are the Ionian Islands off the west coast, the Aegean Islands in the Aegean Sea, and Crete. Greece has over 2,000 islands, but only 170 have people living on them. Many of these islands are the tops of mountains that sank into the sea thousands of years ago.

More than three-quarters of Greece is covered by mountains. The Pindus is our most important mountain range. It runs down the center of Greece like a backbone. Its highest peak, at 2,917 meters (9,570 feet), is Mount Olympus. This is the legendary home of the gods! The rocky mountains of the north are very steep. Narrow, fast-flowing rivers twist through their **gorges**.

We also have many great beaches and quiet sheltered shores. The Oinoussai Pit, off the southern tip of the Peloponnese, is 4,850 meters (15,912 feet) deep. It's the deepest point in the Mediterranean.

The island of Corfu. No one in Greece lives more than about 100 kilometers (62 miles) from a beach!

The island of Anafi. Much of Greece is covered by rocky mountains.

Greece has a mostly moderate climate, because we are surrounded by sea. It is usually not very hot or very cold. The sun shines for 300 days of the year! Our 'rainy season' is from November to February. The northwestern area receives the most rain. Thessaly, in the south, has a continental climate. Its summers are hot and stormy, and its winters are cold. Snow can still be found on the peaks of the Pindus ranges in early summer.

Average temperatures

	January	July
Athens	11°C/52°F	32°C/90°F
Thessaloniki	10°C/50°F	32°C/90°F
Crete	13°C/55°F	33°C/91°F

Plants and animals

About two-thirds of Greece is covered by forest. We have many different types of trees. These include oak, fir, pine, mulberry, palm and fruit trees. Millions of olive trees have been planted in Greece over the centuries.

Wild flowers bloom in the spring and early summer. They cover dry fields and rocky mountains with a carpet of color. We have more types of wild flowers than any other country in Europe. Over 500 of our flowers can be found only in Greece. Many plants like the hyacinth, iris, rose, olive, honeysuckle and the laurel are connected with our ancient myths. Herbs that we use in our cooking, such as oregano, basil, sage and thyme, also grow in the wild here.

The tamarisk plant, with its feathery branches, is native to Greece.

*Greek goats
have curly horns!*

Only a few animals, such as wild boars, wolves and **lynxes**, can still be found in the wild. We have set up national parks to help protect our wildlife. The waters around Zakynthos and Kefallonia are home to one of the few colonies of sea turtles left in Europe. Tortoises are still found on the mainland and islands, and pelicans often land on our shores. Dolphins and porpoises follow our fishing boats. Some of our rare animals can be found only in Greece. White *agrimi* goats and **chamois** live on Crete, and miniature horses live on the island of Skyros.

Cities and landmarks

Athens is the capital of Greece. It was named after Athena, the goddess of wisdom and knowledge. Athens is a huge, noisy, busy city. Over three million people live here, which is about one-quarter of our population. The city has a mix of ancient buildings and modern, high-rise apartment blocks. There are many colorful markets where you can buy almost anything!

The city of Athens became the capital in 1834. Today the ancient parts of the city are surrounded by modern apartment blocks.

The ancient Greeks built their temples to the gods on the top of a steep hill in Athens. This hill was called the Acropolis, which means 'upper city'. The ruins of the Acropolis can be seen from almost everywhere in Athens. There were once huge buildings and statues made of bronze or marble, covered with gold and precious stones. Now only four buildings remain. These include the Parthenon, the Erechtheion, and the ancient theater of Dionysos. This is the oldest theater in the world, and is still used for plays today.

The Parthenon was built almost 2,500 years ago as a temple to the goddess Athena.

Our main port is Piraeus. Like Athens, it was once a small village. Now it is one of the major ports in the Mediterranean. A naval museum and the remains of the Archaeological Museum can be found here. Thessaloniki is our second-largest city. It was founded by Cassander, the brother-in-law of Alexander the Great. He named the city after his wife, who came from Thessaly. Many buildings, such as the Venetian White Tower, are monuments that were constructed by the Romans or Turks. They invaded the city centuries ago.

*Greek soldiers, known as **evzones**, march past the ruins of the Erechtheion on the Acropolis.*

Industry and agriculture

Greece is known more for its agriculture than for its industry. We have few natural resources, and we do not have many heavy industries. However, this has slowly started to change since **World War 2**. The government has helped to support new industries such as food processing and the manufacture of cigarettes, cement, clothing and textiles.

Shipping and ship-building are two of our major industries. Our **merchant navy** is the largest in the world. Some of the world's richest people are Greek ship-owners! Tourism is also good for our economy. Every year, millions of people come here from all over the world. They visit our ancient ruins, eat in our *tavernas*, and soak up the sun on our magnificent beaches.

A fisherman dries his catch of octopus. Many people are employed in the fishing industry, either catching fish or canning it. We have 250 different kinds of fish, including swordfish, perch, lobster and shrimp.

Greece is dry and mountainous, so only one-third of our land is suitable for farming. Our farms are very small. Many farmers still use mules and donkeys, as well as tractors, to help them work the land. Our biggest commercial crops are cotton and tobacco. We also grow wheat, sugar beet, figs, grapes, oranges and lemons. Olive trees love our dry climate, and olives are grown in many different parts of Greece. Some farmers keep bees to make honey. Others keep sheep and goats. **Fetta** cheese and yogurt are popular dairy products.

Olive groves are found in many parts of Greece.

A farmer tends his flock on Crete.

Transportation

Many of the roads in Greece are steep and narrow because we have so many mountains. These roads have sheer cliffs on one side, and a drop to the ocean on the other. People often take buses to travel to the next village or town. Many of our buses are old and crowded, but they are often gaily decorated. Plastic flowers, religious paintings and pictures of the driver's family are used to brighten the buses. There is usually a noisy radio too! You can travel almost anywhere in Greece by bus.

Donkeys are very good at walking over rough, stony ground. Some farmers use donkeys to transport goods.

In our main cities, Athens and Thessaloniki, traffic is a big problem. The many cars clogging the streets cause traffic jams and air pollution. Cars are not allowed on the cobblestone streets of Spetses. People here still use horse-drawn carriages to get around.

Our main port, Piraeus, is an important shipping and financial center. The port links Athens with our many islands and with the rest of the world. People travel out to the islands by ship, ferry or **hydrofoil**. Some families use their own boats to take travellers between the islands.

Our state-owned airline is Olympic Airways. It flies people around the mainland, between islands, and to many countries around the world. We have 9 international and twenty-eight domestic airports around the country.

A hydrofoil takes passengers to the island of Skiathos. Hydrofoils are more expensive than ferries, but they are much faster.

History and government

Five thousand years ago, the island of Crete was home to people known as the Minoans. They were a peaceful people who traded with other countries, and built beautiful cities with 'modern' conveniences. The King's Palace at Knossos had bathtubs, flushing toilets, and hot- and cold-running water! Around 1100 BC, the Minoans mysteriously disappeared. Some historians believe a volcano erupted on a nearby island, causing earthquakes and tidal waves that wiped them out.

Around 1600 BC, a great civilization was built by the Mycenaeans in central Greece. These were skilled craftspeople who built walled palaces and created fine pottery and sculptures. Homer's heroic tale, the *Iliad*, tells the story of the **Trojan War**. It was fought between the people of Mycenae and the people of Troy. The Dorians, a tribe from northern Greece, eventually brought their culture to an end around 1100 BC. The next 300 years were known as Greece's Dark Ages because of the instability of the times.

Work on the Temple of Zeus started around 500 BC. It was finished 700 years later by the Roman emperor Hadrian. Now only ruins are left.

Evzones *guarding Parliament House.*

After the Dark Ages, groups of people began to form small 'city-states'. These included Athens, Corinth and Sparta. Each city-state had its own rules and government. Before long, the city-states were fighting with each other. This made it easier for Philip, king of Macedonia, to conquer Greece in 338 BC. His son, Alexander the Great, took over from him two years later. He extended his father's empire to India.

The Romans invaded Greece in 146 BC. This spelled the end of the Greek empire. For the next 2,000 years, Greece was ruled by people from other countries. The Romans, the **Byzantines** and finally, the Ottoman Turks, all invaded and ruled Greece at different times.

Greece has seen centuries of struggle, including civil war and severe hardship for many of its people. However, modern Greece has a brighter future. Greece became a democratic republic in 1974. The people voted to reject a **monarch** as head of state. They set up a parliamentary democracy instead. This means that the people choose who governs the country.

Fact file

Official name Hellenic Republic		**Population** 10,707,000	**Land area** 131,957 square kilometers (51,463 square miles)

Official name	Hellenic Republic
Population	10,707,000
Land area	131,957 square kilometers (51,463 square miles)
Government	parliamentary republic
Language	Modern Greek
Religions	Christianity (Greek Orthodox 98%, Roman Catholic), Islam
Currency	Drachma (DR) 1 DR = 100 *lepta*
Capital city	Athens
Major cities	Thessaloniki, Piraeus, Patras, Larisa, Iraklion
Number of islands	over 2,000 (only 170 are populated)
Length of coastline	15,000 kilometers (9,321 miles)
Climate	mild wet winters and hot dry summers
Major rivers	Evros, Nestos, Strymon and Axios
Highest mountain	Mount Olympus 2,917 meters (9,571 feet)
Main farm products	wheat, sugar beet, tobacco, cotton, grapes, raisins, olives, olive oil, citrus fruit
Main industries	tourism, clothing, shipping, metal products, processed food, textiles, cement
Natural resources	bauxite, lignite, magnesite, oil, marble

Glossary

Byzantine	relates to the Eastern Roman Empire, AD 395–1453
chamois	a goat-like deer
Classical Period	the time from 475–323 BC, when Greece led the world in arts and sciences
evzones	ceremonial soldiers
fetta	a cheese made from goat's milk
gorges	deep, narrow valleys created by rivers running through mountains
hydrofoil	a fast boat that 'skis' across water
icons	religious pictures of Jesus Christ, or of the saints, painted on wooden panels
Lent	a period of 40 days leading up to Easter, when people fast and repent their sins
lime	a white material, made from a rock called limestone, used for whitewashing houses
lynx	a type of wildcat
merchant navy	commercial ships
monarch	a king, queen or emperor
myths	traditional stories that help to explain events
playwright	a writer of plays
taverna	a bar or restaurant
Trojan War	a 10-year war fought between the Greeks and the people of the city of Troy around 1250 BC
World War 2	a war from 1939 to 1945. The Allies (the United States, the Soviet Union, Britain, France and others) defeated the Axis powers (Germany, Italy and Japan)
Yaya	Grandma

Index

$16.95

DATE			

03

APR 1 0 2002

BAKER & TAYLOR